THRILLING THEME PARKS

SIX FLAGS

BY MONIKA DAVIES

EPIC

EPIC, AN IMPRINT OF BELLWETHER MEDIA BY FLUTTERBEE

EPIC

EPIC BOOKS are no ordinary books. They burst with intense action, high-speed heroics, and shadows of the unknown. Are you ready for an Epic adventure?

This edition first published in 2027 by Bellwether Media, Inc.

For information regarding permission, write to Bellwether Media, Inc., Attention: Permissions Department, 3500 American Blvd W, Suite 150, Bloomington, MN 55431.

Library of Congress Cataloging-in-Publication Data is available at www.loc.gov or upon request from the publisher.

ISBN: 9798898801052 (hardcover)
ISBN: 9798898802295 (ebook)

Editor: Elizabeth Neuenfeldt Designer: Gabriel Hilger

Printed in the United States of America, North Mankato, MN.

TABLE OF CONTENTS

FUN IS CALLING

Two friends ride the Medusa. The ride races at full speed. It twists! It turns!

The friends scream with joy. It is a fun day at Six Flags.

MEDUSA

There are over 20 Six Flags parks. Each one is packed with thrilling rides.

SIX FLAGS MAP

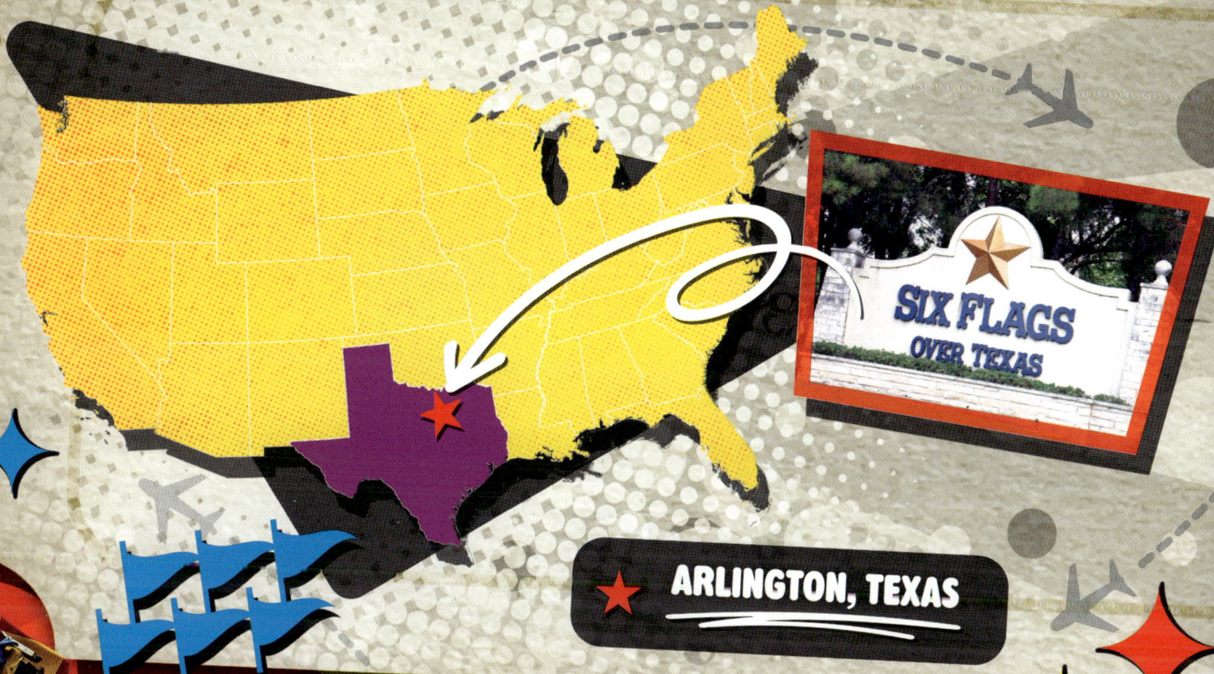

The first park was Six Flags Over Texas. It is in Arlington, Texas. The park is still open today!

THE MAKING OF SIX FLAGS

BORN 1914

ROLE
Founder of Six Flags Over Texas

ACCOMPLISHMENT
Helped build Six Flags parks across the United States

ANGUS G. WYNNE JR.

Disneyland opened in 1955. It was a huge success. People saw how popular it was.

Angus G. Wynne Jr. was a Texan businessman. He went to Disneyland. It **inspired** him to make a **theme park** in Texas.

The park took only a year to **construct**. It opened in 1961. It was named Six Flags Over Texas. It had six themed areas.

People loved Six Flags! Around 17 million people visited the park in the first ten years.

SHORT-TERM PARK

Angus did not plan for the theme park to stay! At first, he only wanted to keep it open for a few years.

The Sidewinder ride opened in 1961. El Aserradero opened in 1963. It was the world's first log **flume** ride!

A PARK OF FIRSTS

Most theme parks charged per ride. But Six Flags was the first park to have one entrance fee.

In 1966, the Runaway Mine Train opened. People still love this exciting ride.

Soon, more locations opened. Six Flags Over Georgia opened in 1967. What became Six Flags Magic Mountain opened in 1971.

Parks were built in other countries too. Six Flags México opened in 2000.

SIX FLAGS OVER GEORGIA

Six Flags Magic Mountain Attendance Records

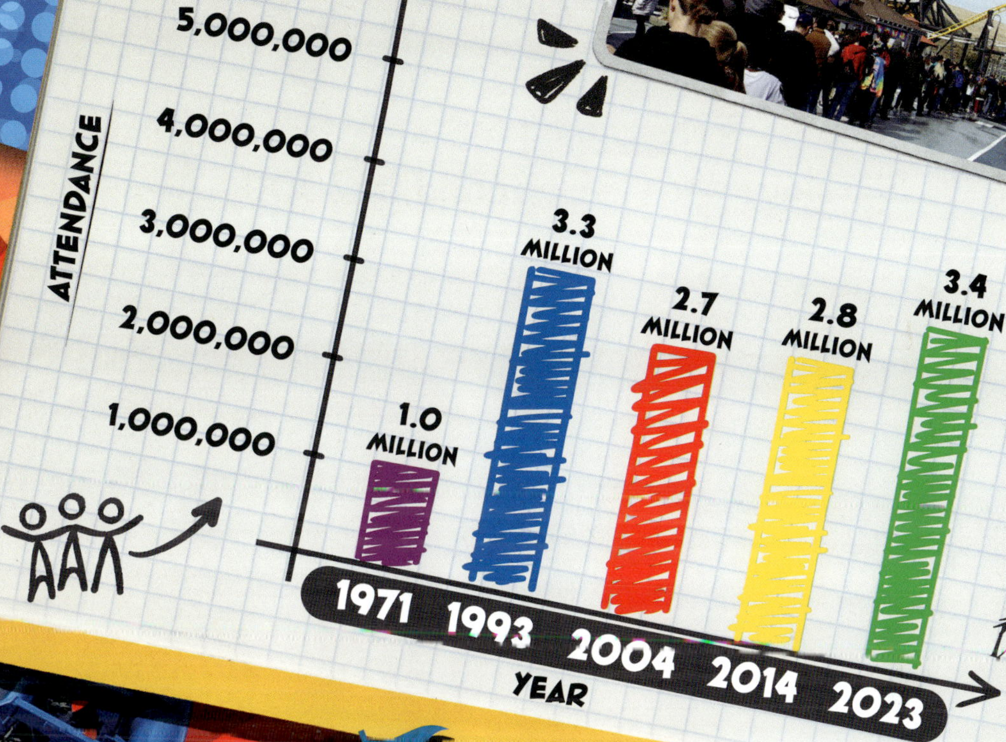

SIX FLAGS MÉXICO

SIX FLAGS TODAY

EL ASERRADERO

Six Flags Over Texas still has themed areas. Riders zoom past scenes on BATMAN The Ride in Gotham City.

FAMOUS SIGHTINGS

Many famous singers first performed at Six Flags. This includes Kelly Clarkson.

El Aserradero is still a popular ride. It is in the Mexico and Spain area.

People can ride the Mini Mine Train in Boomtown. The Oil Derrick tower stands tall in the Tower area.

The Texas area is still the heart of Six Flags. Here, riders zoom on the Titan coaster!

TITAN

WHAT IS IT?

A steel roller coaster

STAT

It reaches speeds of 85 miles (137 kilometers) per hour.

FUN FACT

The ride was once teal and orange. It was repainted to red, white, and blue in 2025.

SIX FLAGS EVENTS

Six Flags hosts Star-Spangled Nights on July 4. People watch fireworks. They listen to music.

Holiday in the Park

DATE

End of November to January

EVENT

This holiday festival has live shows and bright lights!

LOCATIONS

Six Flags Over Texas, Six Flags Fiesta Texas, Six Flags Magic Mountain

Many love to buy **souvenirs** of different rides. Six Flags is a seriously fun time!

Glossary

construct—to build

flume—a sloping channel for carrying water

inspired—gave someone an idea about what to do or create

souvenirs—things people keep as reminders of places they visited

theme park—a park where the rides and shows are based on a certain subject

To Learn More

AT THE LIBRARY

Davies, Monika. *Walt Disney World*. Minneapolis, Minn.: Bellwether Media, 2027.

Duling, Kaitlyn. *Roller Coasters*. Minneapolis, Minn.: Bellwether Media, 2023.

Romero, Libby. *Amusement Park*. New York, N.Y.: DK Publishing, 2023.

ON THE WEB

FACTSURFER

Factsurfer.com gives you a safe, fun way to find more information.

1. Go to www.factsurfer.com.
2. Enter "Six Flags" into the search box and click 🔍.
3. Select your book cover to see a list of related content.

Index

The images in this book are reproduced through the courtesy of: Cassiohabib, front cover, p. 1; Jeremy Thompson/ Wikimedia Commons, front cover, pp. 1, 11, 12, 14, 16-17, 19 (Titan); Pit Stock, front cover, p. 1; Jeremy Thompson/ Flickr, front cover, pp. 1, 3, 13, 19 (sign); Image Professionals GmbH/ Alamy Stock Photo, pp. 2-3; DimiTalen/ Wikimedia Commons, p. 4; Cassiohabi, p. 5; Panagiotis Kotsovolos/ Alamy Stock Photo, p. 6; Q-Images/ Alamy Stock Photo, p. 7; Joanne Wynne/ Wikimedia Commons, p. 8; 999re-al/ Wikimedia Commons, p. 8 (inset); Carol M. Highsmith/ Wikimedia Commons, p. 9; Loadmaster (David R. Tribble)/ Wikimedia Commons, pp. 10, 16 (El Aserradero), 18; Roller Coaster Philosophy/ Wikimedia Commons, p. 15 (attendance); Alex234/ Wikimedia Commons, p. 15 (Six Flags Mexico); Brian Moran/ Flickr, p. 20; Mathew Imaging/ Contributor/ Getty Images, p. 21.